幽默俳句

Humor Haiku

MARGARET ZHAO

Humor Haiku

ISBN: 978-0-692-40493-5

My special thanks and gratitude to my brother Repeat Happiness for his beautiful artwork.

Book design by John Schadegg.

Dedicated with much love
to my family and to your family

Praise

点评

Margaret Zhao, a popular speaker, author and teacher, is a master of haiku poetry. I am one among many Facebook followers who enjoy reading Margaret's humorous haiku posts about life in the USA. Her wit and wisdom are in demand and well accepted by her readers. I am happy to see her unique poems published in a book to reach a wider audience. It is my supreme joy and great honor to endorse this book of haiku poems by Margaret Zhao, an author with a wise mind and a generous heart.

Lillian Nader, Resource Specialist, EdM
Author of "Pandora," a musical comedy

玛格丽特赵是一位备受欢迎的演说家, 作家和教师, 而且也是一位俳句大师。我是她的众多脸书粉丝之一, 阅读欣赏她分享的每一首幽默俳句短诗, 体现美国的生活趣事。她的幽默智慧深受广大读者喜爱。我非常高兴看到她这本风格独特的诗作出版，让更多读者品尝。也是我无比的喜悦和莫大的荣幸挚诚地向读者推荐这本诗集。

莉莲·纳德，资源专家，EdM（教育硕士）

“Pandora” 音乐喜剧作家

✲✲✲

"Margaret Zhao captures with just a few words the essence of the world and our human foibles, mixing in her usual indomitable humor to make you laugh and sometimes cry. Even if you don't usually read poetry, hers is well worth the time."

Ann Bridges，Silicon Valley Writer

寥寥数字，玛格丽特赵就能捕捉到这个世界和人性的优劣之精华，再加上威力无比的幽默，你会笑，偶尔还会哭。即使你不常阅读诗词，可她的诗非常值得欣赏。

安·布里奇斯，硅谷作家

✲✲✲

Margaret Zhao is a talented author and painter of words. Her haiku evokes powerful images of life, beauty and humor. Margaret's poetry stays with me through my day as I go out into the world. She helps me to find the simple joy in observing nature. From her memoir, "Really Enough", to her haiku work, Margaret never disappoints."

Heather S. Friedman Rivera, R.N., J.D., Ph.D. Author of "Healing the Present from the Past," "Quiet Water," "Maiden Flight," and "Into Exaltia."

玛格丽特赵是一位才华出众的作家和文学艺术家。她的作品能激发读者强烈的生命力, 美感和幽默感。玛格丽特的诗歌在生活中能伴随我全天快乐。她帮助我找到如何观察自然朴素的乐趣。从她的回忆录, "Really Enough", 到她的俳句作品, 玛格丽特从来没有令人失望过。

希瑟 S.弗里德曼里维拉, R.N., J.D.博士，著作: “过去治愈现在”, “安静水”, “处女航”等

A writer who understands the human heart, Margaret Zhao is an artist who paints pictures in words. She can convey deep story-telling through powerful imagery. Her work uplifts and inspires and is a pure joy to read. Margaret's new book is a “must read”.

Dr. Marjorie Miles, DCH, MFT,
Author of “Healing Haikus” – A Poetic Prescription for Surviving Cancer”

玛格丽特赵是一位理解读者心理的作家, 也是善用文字描绘图像的艺术家。她能自由朴实地表达故事意味深长的画面。她的作品画面美与艺术妙笔融为一体, 使人振奋鼓舞, 是纯粹的赏心悦目。玛格丽特的新书 “必读”。

玛乔丽·迈尔斯, DCH, MFT 博士,著有 “医治俳句”

PREFACE

前言

The following are three simple poetic limericks, which I first heard in China when I was a young girl and have proved to be a major influence in my life. Though not penned by famous poets, they all contain special messages which are cornerstones in my life.

The first one is a poem about a five year old little girl, who suffered a skin disease which left her right eye deformed from the growth of the painful boils on the upper and lower lids. With the eye stretched grotesquely, she was called Pulled Eye Lid. As a result, this less than flattering nick name brought forth a poem:

Pulled Eye Lid selling chestnuts
Peddling to the city streets
For elder sister to eat.

My siblings and I chanted it like a song for years. Never was I aware that it was demeaning or offensive as that little girl happened to be me! So far, no one has claimed the authorship.

The second poem is a poem my mother had me recite many times. The significance of this poem is about snow without mentioning the word snow. The vivid way it described the snow was hilarious to me then, and still is:

The world is a blur
And the well a frozen hole
A yellow dog turns white,
A white dog grows fat.

The laughter my mother and I shared from this limerick was unforgettable. It was one of the few pleasures available to us.

The third poem is a limerick that came with a little story my mother made sure I was able to retell a thousand times:

Long long ago in old China on a summer day, there were three strangers waiting under a big tree to cross the river. Among them were two men and one woman. One of the men was a Literary Scholar, and the other was a Military Officer. As for the woman, she happened to be just a middle aged housewife with bound feet.

As the wooden canoe needed time to come over from the other side of the river, one of the men thought of a plan to kill time and play a trick on the woman. He suggested: "Since we are just waiting here with nothing else to do, shall we play a game? And the one who loses will pay the fares for the three of us." All agreed. So, the same man continued, "We can compose a poem, requiring the use of the words: Pointed, Rounded, while ending the poem with an important rank." With that being said, he took the lead to present his:

"My brush is pointed
and my ink-tray rounded
with my profound knowledge
I become a Literary Scholar"

Then it was the other man's turn,

"My arrow is pointed
and my bow rounded
with my solid strength
I become a Military Officer"

The woman calmly took a moment to think and accepted her turn,

"My feet are pointed
and my belly rounded
with one pregnancy born two rascals
one becomes a Literary Scholar, the other a Military Officer"

As a result, the woman won because she positioned herself as their mother figure, which in Chinese culture is a humorous way to assert one's advantage to outwit another.

I still find this limerick funny and pleasurable. More importantly I find it incredibly empowering.

These three poems have enriched my life in many ways and have caused me to have enduring interest in poetry of all kinds.

After I came to America, I encountered a Japanese form of poetry with three lines and seventeen syllables called Haiku. I find the style of Haiku very humorous and stimulating obligating the writer to use only limited lines and words to express profundity. I have started to write Haiku poetry with my own style - it is gushing out of me in torrents now as follows:

among those keen thoughts
speaking so beautifully is
the voice of Haiku

Chinese have a famous saying to indicate that smile can make one look young and beautiful:

one smile
ten years
younger

I consider it a great reward when I see my Haiku bring my readers a laugh, a smile, or a thought provoking pause. I hope you enjoy them. And wishing you,

many smiles
infinite years
younger

当我还是一个不谙世故的小女孩的时候, 我在国内最初邂逅的以下三首打油诗予我未来的生活以极大的影响。虽然不是出于著名诗人之笔, 但它们所具有的独特深刻含义, 成为我生活情趣的奠基石。

第一首诗是关于一个五岁左右小女孩的诗。因患一种皮肤病, 她右眼的上眼睑和下眼睑各长着疼痛不已的脓胞疮。痊愈后的脓胞疮留下的疤痕使她的右眼上下拉扯变形, 因此而获一诨名: 扯眼皮。也正是这一不太褒奖的诨名成就了一首诗:

扯眼皮卖板栗

卖到街市里

给大姐吃

我的兄弟姐妹和我吟诵了好些年, 就像唱歌一样。而我丝毫也没意识到其贬低或不恭的意思, 因为那个小女孩就是我自己! 到目前为止, 还没有作者声称著作版权。

第二首诗, 我母亲常常让我背诵。这首诗的经典意义在于它是一首关于雪的诗, 可只字不提雪字。其生动的雪景描绘使得当时的我感到特别的幽默有趣, 现在仍是如此:

江山一笼统

井口一窟窿

黄狗身变白

白狗身变肿

这首打油诗给我和母亲带来的欢笑令我至今难以忘怀。也是当时我们仅有的一点点快乐。

第三首诗是一个小故事。母亲让我讲上千百遍：

相传很久以前, 盛夏的一天, 在渡口河畔的一颗大树下有三个等着过河的人, 他们分别是两男一女。其间一个是文官一个是武官, 那女子只是个普通的家庭妇女。因为摆渡的小木船还远在对岸不能马上过来, 为了排遣等船的寂寞和无聊还想故意戏弄一下那个裹足的女子, 其中一人提议道: "反正现在咱们等船无事倒不如做个游戏小赌一下, 谁输了谁承付三人的过河船钱, 如何？" 那俩人一听同时点头应允表示愿意, 这个就又说了: "咱们作诗, 以"尖尖""圆圆"为头两句的结尾, 第四句的最后一字以"元"结束。说罢 自己为头作了一首:

"我笔儿尖尖

砚台圆圆

凭着满腹的学识

我考上了文状元"

轮到了另一个男子, 他即刻应道：

“我剑儿尖尖

弓儿圆圆

凭借扎实的功底

我考上了武状元”

最后只剩下了这个少妇了, 她不慌不忙略沉吟了一下答道：

“我脚儿尖尖

肚儿圆圆

一胎生两个

一个文状元一个武状元”

结果, 少妇获胜。因为声称自己为他人之母是占便宜的意思, 是中国文化的一种幽默。

时至当今, 我仍然觉得这首诗趣味无穷。更重要的一点, 我觉得这首诗给予我非常的精神激励。

这三首诗在很多方面都丰富了我的生活，引起我对各种诗歌产生持久的兴趣。

来到美国之后，我接触到一种日本短诗，其格式是三句十七个音节称之为俳句。我发现这种诗的形式非常幽默且有挑战性，要求作者用有限的句子和音节来表达深刻的寓意。

于是我开始创作自己自由形式的俳句。此时也如潮水涌泉如下：

文思纷繁
那甜美的声音
来自俳句

中国有句名言, 声称笑容可以使人年轻美丽：

笑一笑

十年

少

我感到最为欣慰的就是当我的短诗带给我的读者欢笑，微笑，或瞬间的停顿感悟。希望您也喜欢。

并祝您，

多笑笑

万年

少

Contents

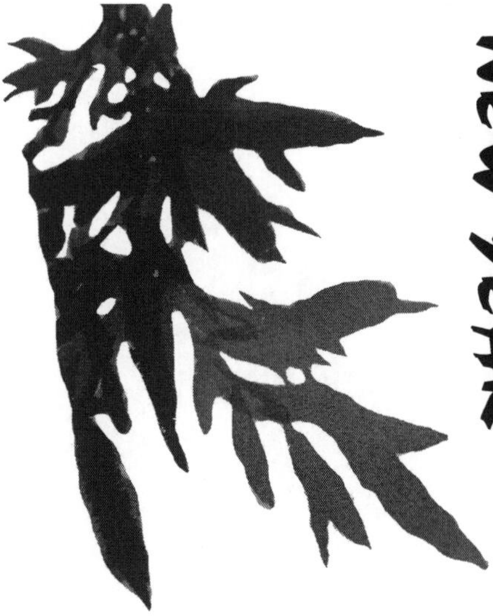

NEW YEAR

新年

that one tick
of the clock provokes
the new year's knock

正是那一嘀嗒

的钟声惹来了

新年的敲门声

all of us aboard
new year's sailing vessel
be your own Captain

我们共同登上

新年的航班

您自己当船长

awakened after midnight
by the bright moonlight
shining since last year

惊醒午夜后

明月闪耀着

去年的光辉

without much effort
we just won the second
day of the new year

不费吹灰之力

我们就赢得了

新年的第二天

a whiff of scent
from the rose apple candle
breathing out first breath

清香扑鼻

来自玫瑰苹果蜜蜡烛

那第一口气

SPRING

春

the red rose
speaking spring with lips fragrant
is my favorite

那朵红色玫瑰

香唇说着春天的话语

是我的最爱

in a sea of red
an outstanding addition
that yellow tulip

在一片红色的海洋里

锦上添花的

是那朵黄色郁金香

an outburst of blooms
and clamorous birds
awake last winter's twigs

怒放的春色

和喧闹的小鸟

吵醒了冬眠的枯枝

racing to bloom
in the afternoon warmth
uproarious roses

竞相争艳

绽放在温暖午后

喧嚷的玫瑰

sprays of aroma
intoxicate me and the bees,
from kumquat flowers

飘洒的芳香

醉昏了我和蜜蜂

来自金桔花

wild daisies
smile from petal to petal
contagiously

野雏菊

一片片花瓣

传染着微笑

taming my hair,
I watch poppies ripple
in wind

一手驯服我的头发

一边观赏罂粟花

风中荡漾

a stroll of leisure
after the rain with every step
stepping on spring

闲情散步

在雨后

步步踩着春色

an evening primrose
blooms as the moon rising
scent of quietude

报春花

绽开在月亮升起之际

寂静的謦香

roses are glamorous
while a gardenia's aroma
nonpareil

玫瑰花妩媚不已

而栀子花芳香

无比

morning glories
tooting their trumpets
quietly

牵牛花

扬起嘟嘟喇叭

悄无声息

kempt hair unkempt
in a gust of spring wind
fingers used as a comb

整齐的头发乱蓬蓬

一阵春风撩过

手指当梳子

sounding rain last night
wetting my wooden fence where
I watch quails sashay

昨夜雨声急

湿透的木栅栏

是我欣赏鹌鹑走秀的地方

my yellow scarf
dripping wet
of spring shower

我的黄围巾

湿透了

春天的阵雨

spring sky rains noodles
blown aslant by morning wind
smearing my window

春天空中降面条

被晨风吹得歪歪斜斜

涂抹我的窗户

zong zi - sweet rice wrapped
in bamboo leaves, memorial
to an ancient poet

粽子-

糯米包在竹叶里

纪念古代诗人

after the spring rain,
the grass is greener
than before

春雨过后

绿草

更绿

SUMMER

夏

pumpkin seeds dwindled
while drying under the sun,
a mouse caught red handed

晒太阳的南瓜籽

所剩无几

作案的是小老鼠

summer's fiery ball
slips to the ocean sizzling,
a cause of heat waves

夏日的火球

滑落海洋丝丝响

掀起热浪

palm trees are branchless
with leaves perfect for fans
fanning in the air

棕树无分枝

天然的扇子是棕树的叶子

在空中摇曳

free acupunctures
by the lake after sunset,
mosquitoes' needles

免费针灸
在夕阳后的湖畔
蚊子的针

heated summer clouds
seeing themselves in a pool
for a cooling bath

夏天酷热的云朵

俯览自己在游泳池

泡凉澡

awakened pine trees
drenched in the brew of sunrise
with eyelashes on fire

惊醒的松树

浸泡在燃烧的朝霞里

睫毛也着了火

a straw hat
transmuted into a kite
by swirl wind

草帽

变成了风筝

在漩涡风中

follows me closely
a shadow in broad daylight
from my parasol

光天化日之下

紧随我的黑影

来自我的阳伞

glossy lips ajar
tulips sing perennially
scented songs of love

玉唇半开合

郁金香常年不懈地

唱着沁心的爱情之歌

hibernating
in summer
my long red coat

冬眠

在夏天

我的红色长大衣

my friend asks me
in the middle of a drought
for a rain check

正值干旱之际

朋友请我

改期

parched hills breathe sweet green
after a long wait for the rain
to the bitter end

焦灼的山丘呼吸甜美的绿色
饱经苦苦的等待
雨季才到来

the clouds are at a loss
when the wind stops blowing
across the crossroads

行云不知所措

当风停歇在

十字路口

in broad stillness
the moon looking at herself
in every lake

万籁寂无声

明月自我观赏

在每一个湖中

a sand castle comes
to life with dripping sweat
from a topless boy

沙塔大功告成

汗流浃背

小男孩赤膊上阵

AUTUMN

秋

in a far distance
I first spot on the way home
yellow chrysanthemum

远在回乡的路上

最先映入我的眼帘

金菊花

autumn wind
fanning my neighbor's maple tree
ablaze

秋风

扇红邻居的梧桐树

如火如荼

silent as the grave
the trees kiss off their leaves and bow
art of detachment

寂静得像墓地

树木吻别树叶再鞠躬

放手的艺术

single handedly
pregnant with many babies
a full figured pumpkin

单枪匹马

怀孕多胎婴儿

大腹便便的南瓜

tapping the windshield,
a fallen leaf's ride on wind
takes a speedy break

敲了敲车窗

一片风驰的落叶

疾速地停顿了片刻

a leftover dish
with barely enough hot sauce
this late autumn sun

余下的一只盘
盛着所剩不多的辛辣味
晚秋的太阳

lurid fallen leaves
cuddle a lone wooden bench
sharing warm reminiscence

斑斓的落叶

拥着孤单的长木椅

同忆昔日温暖

to be chilly, or
not to be chilly banks on
autumn's moodiness

冷不冷

依仗

秋日的情绪

autumn's abrupt blast
shakes a tree of leaves with birds
to panic flight

秋风摇木

栖息的树叶与鸟

落荒而逃

a free cruise
for the fallen leaves
after it rained cats and dogs

免费乘游轮

只为落叶

大雨过后

red lanterns dangle
bursting laughs with teeth mouthful
ripened pomegranates

红灯晃悠悠

大笑露出满口牙

熟透的石榴

China's autumn tiger
America's Indian summer
same lingering heat

中国的秋老虎

美国的小阳春

同样挥之不去的炎热

as days grow shorter
owls burning more
midnight oil

白昼渐短

夜猫子更是

挑灯夜战

冬 WINTER

an arctic storm
swept North Pole to doorsteps
turning houses to glaciers

北极风暴

席卷北极上门

房屋变冰川

winter morning sun
greeting a lonely oak tree,
heard by distant mountains

冬日的朝阳

问候凄清的橡树

被远山听见

the squirrel I missed
over the chilly wintry days
appears with his bride

我惦念的松鼠

寒冷的冬日之后

携新娘露面

a magnolia leaf
lying quietly underfoot
slowly curls in cold

玉兰叶

静静地躺在脚下

寒冷中慢慢卷起

crooked branches of oak trees
with angel fingers spreading
uphold winter chills

弯弯曲曲的橡树枝

犹如天使张开的手指

托着冬季的严寒

good benefits
on a cold snowy day
hot flashes

福利

在寒冷的雪天

潮热

glory of the night
wearing thin in the morning
full or waned, the same moon

夜晚风光黎明微光

无论是圆还是缺

同是一个月亮

on a wooden bench
rests a sojourner under
tender leafless trees

长木椅上

歇着跋涉的路人

光杆枝条树垂下轻柔

after the snow storm
breathless cars transmogrified
into white cocoons

雪灾之后

毫无气息的车辆

变成白蚕茧

mischievously,
a snowman stands
upside down

淘气

雪人站立

脚朝天头朝地

bony branches of trees
plumped up to plump icicles
glistening in light

骨瘦枝条

摇变丰腴冰柱

熠熠闪光

BEAUTY

美

enjoy watching
my shadow in sunset,
what a slim body!

欣赏自己

夕阳下的长影

好秀气的身段!

a splash of moonlight
whitewashed me with my blanket
and my beauty sleep

月光如注

染白了我和被褥

还有我的美人眠

crowned as superstars
donned in gold yellow crimson
Chinese pistache trees in the west

加冕为超级巨星

身着万紫千红

中国黄连木树在西方

a happy face is
beauty one can own without
costing a fortune

喜乐的容颜

美丽妩媚

不需高花费

fountain of beauty
cascading from the face
that wears a smile

美丽的源泉

漫溢在

戴着微笑的脸庞

a majestic stroke
across the sky to mountain tops
appears the rainbow

气派无比的画笔

从天穹到山顶

一弯彩虹

iridescent clouds
woven into fine art hung
on the horizon

彩云

编织成精美的艺术品

挂在地平线上

between the blue sky
and a silent road standing
a row of trees

蓝的天

静的路

中间夹着一排树

sound of music
in the bamboo forest
from many flutes

音乐之声

在竹林里

好多的笛子

节日

HOLIDAYS

being not good at cooking
makes one good at driving
on Thanksgiving day

不会烹饪

就得擅长开车

赶上感恩节那一顿

sucked in and spat out
are shoppers by the mall, last
chance on Christmas Eve

商场吞吐购物客

最后时机

除夕之夜

shopping makes
a fat wallet thin and
a thin wallet disappear

购物

肥胖的钱包消瘦

消瘦的钱包消失

lying flat on the lawn
are Santa Claus and his reindeer,
dog tired from working night shift

躺卧在草地上

圣诞老人和他的驯鹿，

晚班劳累之极

m y daughter's visit
along with her entourage
best Mother's Day gift

我女儿的访问

伴随着她的随行人员

最好的母亲节礼物

after the gifts open,
discarded are the wrapping paper
and the surprises

礼物拆开后

扔掉的是包装纸

和惊喜

west Valentine falls
on east Lantern Festival
with love and with light

西方的情人节

正赶上东方的灯会

满了爱满了光

little flags whisper
gratitude of one nation
on Memorial Day

小小的国旗轻声细语

全国人民的追思谢意

在国丧节里

no matter how much
we honor our veterans,
honor them more

无论赋予

退伍军人多少荣誉

再加倍

behind the terror
of each mask, a happy face
enjoys Halloween

恐怖面具的后面
藏着一张兴奋的脸
乐在万圣节

one night's loot lasts days
scary costumes to retire
rest for the wicked

一晚战利品数日享受

吓人装束下岗

恶人休息

ANIMALS

动物

two little lizards
flex muscles in my backyard
doing push-ups fast

两只小蜥蜴

在我的后院炫耀肌肉

匆匆做起俯卧撑

brownish walnuts
rolling down the hill in wind
a brood of baby quails

棕色核桃

随风滚下山

一窝小鹌鹑

a white egret strolls
along a quiet lake to watch
the sky in water

一只白鹭

悠闲逛湖边

水中观天

sudden departure
of startled geese left behind
plowed waves

野鹤惊飞起

留下一片

犁过的波浪

wild pond
mandarin ducks
a splashing rendezvous

野塘

鸳鸯

水溅幽会涧

slanted yellow eyes
a cat's moment of thinking
to prey or not prey

斜眯着黄眼睛

猫的片刻思忖

捕不捕

baby giraffe yawns
swallowing the setting sun
accidentally

小小长颈鹿打哈欠

一不小心

吞下了落日

in a dog park
I see more people
than dogs

在宠狗公园里

我看到的人

比狗多

without a word
my dog lured me to the park,
with just a leash in his mouth

一言不发

狗就把我引诱到公园

皮带衔在口里

a bone shaped cookie
enticing my dog to take
with me a selfie

骨形饼干

讨好我的狗

跟我一起自拍照

fuzzy little balls
in one hidden basket
soon to fly away

绒绒的小球

窝在一只深藏的篮子里

很快就要飞走了

bright red with black spots
a lady bug's dainty wings
tucked into a dot

红色鲜艳黑斑黑

一只瓢虫的轻盈翅膀

塞进一个点

weighing down a branch
of the crabapple tree,
a squirrel is feasting

被压弯的

海棠树枝头

松鼠在美餐

there is one peanut
left behind by the blue jay
empty with seeds gone

一颗花生

被冠蓝鸦留下

空壳不见花生米

in mid air afloat
a hummingbird, blurring wings
barely visible

蜂鸟空中浮

翅膀朦胧

若影若现

a hasty fly bumps
into the glass door, loud bang
for a small body

仓促飞行的苍蝇

撞在玻璃门上

微小的身体碰得声响

birds fan their wings
refusing to drink water
till I disappear

鸟的翅膀扇扇子

拒绝喝水

一直等到我消失

to check the traffic
sticking out of the window
a dog's hairy head

视察一下路况

伸出窗口的

是狗毛茸茸的头

lying on his back,
eyes half open and half closed
a dog's beg for a scratch

四肢朝天仰卧

眼睛半睁半闭

狗的乞求骚一骚痒

morning dawn finds me eating
early breakfast in the dark,
dog's snore undisturbed

晨昏伴我早餐

免得开灯

打扰狗的鼾声

lining on the lamp post
are birds watching the neighborhood
and gossiping

鸟儿排队在电线杆上

观察周边邻舍

搬嘴弄舌

demonstrating Tai Chi,
I caught a spectator yawning
but not barking yet

正示范着太极

却发现一观众打哈欠

好在还没狂吠

RELATIONSHIPS

婚姻爱情

failed relationships
from the past have me realize
it was all their fault

失败婚恋的教训

使我自己终于意识到

尽是他们的错

a leafless branch quavers
singly after the bird has
left for another tree

还在颤抖的

唯独那枝无叶的树枝

小鸟早已移情别的枝头

falling in love
needs no excuses,
but falling out, nothing but

坠入爱河

不需要借口

可分道扬镳, 全是

the pain of lost love
has left hanging
on the weeping willows

失恋的痛苦

之别挂在

垂柳上

alone in the woods,
a quiet path winding to leave
my lost thoughts behind

独步丛林中

蜿蜒寂静的小径

将我的愁绪抛在脑后

happiness is to
discover a prize together
and prize each other

幸福是

共同发现奖品

相互奖励

singing aloud in
the shower, then he realized
he just got married

淋浴时放声歌唱

可突然记起

自己是已婚之夫

peeling the onion
one layer after another
family issues

剥洋葱

一层层

家里那些事

my husband works hard
to bring home the bacon
but I am a vegetarian

丈夫卖力工作

养家糊口

可我只吃素

it surprisingly
dawned to my husband,
finding my iPad finds me

惊讶不已

我丈夫悟出一个道理,

找到 iPad 找到我

NEW DISCOVERY

新发现

bills do not seem to
ever suffer a delay
by the traffic jams

账单似乎

从不遭受

交通堵塞的延误

long missing earrings
showing up in a shoe box
now the shoes are missing

久违的耳环

出现在鞋盒里

鞋子又不见了

I am a diamond
not in the rough
but in my fantasies

我是一颗钻石

不在尚未开凿的顽石中

而在我的幻想里

working can be
interesting, specially so when
watching others

工作其乐无穷

尤其是

看别人工作

without breathing air
no man can live very long
or swear as much

若不呼吸空气

没有哪个男人能活得久

也脏话难出口

long wait in a doctor's office
causes patients to forget
their ailments

医生诊所的久等

等得病人

忘了自己的病

self healing is hard work,
every minute
on the job

养病辛苦

每分钟

都在劳累

illness,
comes like a lion
out like a lamb

病来

如山倒

病去像抽丝

thick fog this morning
failed to quiet the lawn mower
from next door neighbor

早晨的浓雾

掩不住割草机的噪音

来自隔壁邻居

staying at friend's home
makes me feel at home
without homely chores

朋友家

温暖如家

家务不愁

easily aging
hardly wiser, any shortcut
to enlightenment?

衰老容易智慧难长

是否有开悟的

捷径？

glutton for punishment
to self grow organic vegetables
wound up with wild weeds

自讨苦吃

劳作种植有机蔬菜

长出野草来

applying lipstick
without a mirror turns my face
to pink monkey butt

抹口红不照镜子

满嘴涂成

粉红色的猴子屁股

at the funeral
solemn face greets the solemn.
a ghost of a smile

在葬礼上

肃穆的脸招呼肃穆的脸

挂着一丝微笑的魂

paper cut causing
involuntary cursing
pains a finger twice

纸张划破手指

诅咒脱口而出

两次伤其痛处

irresistible fortune
in fortune cookies can be
entertaining or irritating

诱人的预测

在幸运酥饼里

有的可喜有的可恶

rumors
spread
by spicy wind

谣言四起

来自于

辛辣的风

a lie
requires
no rough draft

谎言

不要求

打草稿

many words coming
out of the mouth cloud the mind
as well as the air

口若悬河

迷茫心窍

还有空气

after the party,
crowded
is the dishwasher

聚会之后
最拥挤的
是洗碗机

a dead redwood tree
giving many births
to toothpicks

死去的红杉树

孕育出许多新生命

牙签

the whistle of the teapot
excites a rush
to the stove

茶壶哨声

催促一阵匆忙

赶到火炉旁

socks no telling
right from left,
fitting either foot just right

袜子不分左右

随便穿哪只

都正好

that missing twin
of my favorite socks appears
as a ball in my pants

我喜爱的那双袜子
一只不翼而飞
变成球钻进裤筒

I am looking for
that tunnel with light
at the end

我在寻找

柳暗花明

蹊径

into water
my shadow drops
without a ripple

掉到水里的

是我的身影

不溅一丝涟漪

a tough journey for
self growth, I find myself still
lactose intolerant

自我成长旅程艰难

我发现自己仍有

乳糖不耐症

where there is long line,
there are necks
stretching long

哪里排长队

哪里的脖子

就伸得长

white cotton candy
toothsome
made not from cotton

棉花糖

可口

不含棉花

noodles
are more slippery
when hungry

面条

更滑

在饥饿时

a mother's great happiness
when finally working her baby
to a burp

母亲喜出望外

终于拍出

婴孩一个嗝

meat on dinner table
was living a life,
and then...

餐桌上的肉

原来过着自己的日子

后来...

in rush hours
cars are rushing
hardly

高峰时段

路上的车辆

几乎纹丝不动

detours are
opportunities to get lost
knowingly

辗转绕道

迷路的机会

有意

the reason I got lost
many times in my own neighborhood
has to be someone else's fault

多次迷路

在自己的社区

原因一定是某人的错

LIVING

生活

embrace a new day
by getting out of bed
on the right side

拥抱新的一天

从起床开始

就别怠误

a watched pot
never boils until
I look away

看着的水壶

烧不开水

我得转移视线

a cup of hot tea
to slow down the morning rush
one sip at a time

沏一杯热茶

缓解清晨的匆忙

慢慢品尝

shadow short, shadow long
shadow confused
when I danced

影子短, 影子长

我一跳舞

影子乱成一团

practice of Tai Chi
causing vision to a blur
from steaming glasses

练太极

导致视野模糊,

热气腾腾的眼镜

sitting in a class
to learn about stocks but
they speak only bulls and bears!

坐在教室里

听股票投资讲座

人家尽说什么牛还有熊

talking back to the radio
evokes heated arguments
alone all the way

回应电台话题

挑起激烈舌战

一路就自己

all night I was looking
hard for my missing glasses
till I woke up exhausted

彻夜寻找着

我丢失的眼镜

直到醒来筋疲力尽

a trashed plastic bag
caught by a car on the freeway
flapping like a flag

废弃的塑料袋

乘上高速汽车

像一面旗子飘扬

under the hood of
my skull, housed are racing thoughts
going no places

在我的脑骨盖下

奔腾的思绪

没出息

praying at night for
waking up with enlightenment,
the "waking up" part works

晚间祈祷

愿一觉醒来智慧开悟

"醒来"倒是如愿以偿

talking on the phone
to drive the message across,
nonstop with hand gestures

打电话,

强调起见

手势不停

people wearing holes
in their pants with extra price
make me wonder

人们不惜高价

穿上窟窿裤子

令人不解

smuggled indoors
legally by wind - dust,
creating jobs

随风走私

依法入室 - 灰尘

创造工作机会

a couch potato
quitting the couch,
a long day

沙发懒虫

放弃沙发

好累的一天

the mirror fails to see
the white frost
creeping upon my hair

镜子不见

白霜

爬到我头上

the first woman
landed on Mars last night,
sci-fi peppered my dream

第一位妇女

昨晚登上了火星

科幻回味在梦中

tumbling dryer
spitting out laundry
with hot breath

烘干机

吐出烤干的衣物

满口冒热气

made it to the conference,
best seats all available
but a week too early

终于赶到会场

最好的座位随意挑选

只是一周太早

wake up to drink coffee
or drink coffee to wake up,
a free country

清醒了喝咖啡

还是喝咖啡清醒

尊便

on the train,
I watch people busy
watching their phones

在火车上

我看乘客忙着

看他们的手机

awake from a nap,
it is already dark
now what shall I do?

一觉醒来

天都黑了

那该如何是好？

the panic button
is the key to the car when it is
missing in parking lot

那个恐慌键

是关键

停车场找车

after the wind dies,
there is no funeral
necessary

为逝去的风
没有举行
葬礼的必要

I know myself - not
the greatest driver on the road
but great with chopsticks

自知

不是开车是高手

筷子却不在话下

a fake smile
is happier than
an authentic frown

强装的微笑

比真诚紧皱的眉头

快乐些

one smile
ten years
younger

笑一笑

十年

少

WISHING YOU

many smiles
infinite years
younger

祝您

多笑笑

万年

少

Acknowledgements

后记

With deepest gratitude I would like to thank:

Arnold Bernstein, for his devoted support and unconditional love; Bright Yuan Kellogg for her great knowledge and advice;

Ann Bridge, who spent much of her valuable time reading each of my poems with edits and encouragement;

David Collander, for his wonderful timely feedback;

Kathleen Martens, Laura Navarro, Eunice Fung and Francoise Alexander, for sharing laughs and insight with me;

Lilian Nader, Heather Rivera, Marjorie Miles and Heather Hammer, for their great knowledge and inspiration;

and for those generous friends that have left me comments and liked almost every posting I shared online:

Marion Billington, Faith Harper Trotman, Barbara Kellerman, Kim Anne Brooks-Ondeck, Margaret Molenkamp, Linda Wong, Asher Daniel, Kathy Reed Narum, Karen Barberio-Kitts, Mark Rigor, Afsi Mostajab, Susan M. Jamison, Carol Kellogg, Kelly Cousins, Ela Corcoran, Lily Weng, Sameem Saadat, Carol Hansen, Kathryn Hansen, Carol Graham, Russell Burns, Fran Cassell, Jeanne Lish, Leila Deliman, Jane Lake, Lynne Turbie Menon, Imelda Armstrong, Lia Venet, Linda Porter, and many more that I can't include here because of limited space, and please know my gratitude to you is unlimited.

Sincerely your friend,
Margaret

Author Bio
作家简介

Margaret Zhao is an author and poet, born in Hubei China. She immigrated to the USA in 1989. In collaboration with her co-author, Kathleen Martens, Margaret wrote her first book “Really Enough”, winner of the Sharp Writ Book Award, 2012 for Best Biography /Memoir. Her natural sense of humor has led her to be a Standup Comedian and Motivational Speaker applauded by audience of all ages. She lives in the San Francisco area, where she actively teaches and shares Chinese culture and Buddhist philosophy.

玛格丽特赵, 美籍华人, 祖籍中国湖北公安, 当代作家、诗人, 1989 年移居美国, 现居旧金山。主要作品有回忆录《Really Enough》, 荣获 Sharp Writ Book Award, 2012 年传记类一等奖, 合著作家 凯瑟琳马丁。玛格丽特的幽默天赋使她成为备受观众欢迎的幽默演说家。近年来, 她还积极开展中国传统文化和佛教推广工作, 搭建中美文化交流平台。